BOSTON
THEN & NOW

Thunder Bay Press
An imprint of the Advantage Publishers Group
5880 Oberlin Drive
San Diego, CA 92121-4794
www.thunderbaybooks.com

Produced by PRC Publishing, The Chrysalis Building,
Bramley Road, London W10 6SP, United Kingdom

An imprint of Chrysalis Books Group plc

ISBN-13: 978-1-57145-177-4
ISBN-10: 1-57145-177-3

Library of Congress Cataloging-in-Publication Data
McNulty, Elizabeth, 1971-
      Boston then and now / Elizabeth McNulty.
         p.   cm. -- (Then and now ; 2)
      ISBN 1-57145-177-3
      1. Boston (Mass.) Pictorial works. 2. Boston (Mass.)--History
Pictorial works.   I. Title. II. Title: Boston then and now.
III. Series: Then and now (San Diego, Calif.) ; 2.
   F73.37.M38 1999
   974.4'61'00222--cd21

Printed in China
   7 8 9 10 11 09 08 07 06 05

Acknowledgments:
Thanks to Doug Southard at the Bostonian Society for all his help.
To Jane Holtz Kay for her words of encouragement at our fortuitous
meeting. To Simon Clay for great photography (and detective work) in
the bitter cold. Special thanks to Ann Ghublikian, who first suggested
this project; to JoAnn Padgett for a superb job of editing; and to Allen
Orso for helpful advice. Finally, thanks to David Bacon for all his loving
support and enthusiasm.

For my parents, Jim and Pat, who inspired my love of history and architecture

Picture credits:

The publisher wishes to thank the following for their kind permission to
reproduce the photography for this book:

Front cover image courtesy of Corbis/Bettmann;
The front flap image (bottom), pages 2, 6-7 (bottom), 9, 11, 13, 15, 17, 19,
21, 23, 25, 27, 29, 31, 33, 35, 37 (both), 39, 41, 43, 45, 47, 49, 51, 53, 55, 57,
59, 61, 63, 65, 67, 69, 71, 73, 75, 77, 79 (both), 81, 83, 85, 87, 89, 91, 93, 95,
97, 99, 101 (both), 103, 105, 107, 109, 111 (both), 113, 115, 117, 119, 121,
123, 125, 127, 129, 131, 133, 135, 137, 139, 141, 143, the back cover image
and the back flap image (bottom), courtesy of Simon Clay;
The front flap image (top), pages 1, 4, 6-7 (top), 8, 10, 12, 14, 16, 18, 20, 22,
24, 26, 28, 30, 32, 34, 36, 38, 40, 42, 44, 46, 48, 50, 52, 54, 56, 58, 60, 62, 64,
66, 68, 70, 72, 74, 76, 78 (both), 80, 82, 84, 86, 88, 90, 92, 94, 96, 98 (both),
100, 102, 104, 106, 108, 110, 112 (both), 114, 116, 120, 124, 126, 128, 130,
132, 134, 136, 140, 142 and the back flap image (top), courtesy of The
Bostonian Society;
Page 118 courtesy of the John Fitzgerald Kennedy Library.
Page 138 (both) courtesy of the Boston Public Library Print Department..

Above. Aftermath of the Great Fire of 1872 viewed from Washington Street (*lower left corner*). Covering an area from Summer
Street to State and from Washington to the waterfront, the blaze destroyed almost everything, even leaping from land to claim
wooden sailing ships in the harbor. The Old South Meeting House (*left*) still stands, narrowly saved by the heroic efforts of firefighters and volunteers. Today, this area comprises Downtown Crossing (pages 78–79) and Boston's financial district (pages 50-55).

Page One Photo: Beacon Street looking toward Somerset Street, 1889 (see page 104).

Page Two Photo: Upper Beacon Steet, today (see page 105).

BOSTON
THEN & NOW

ELIZABETH McNULTY

THUNDER BAY
P·R·E·S·S

San Diego, California

INTRODUCTION

We say the cows laid out Boston. Well, there are worse surveyors," wrote Ralph Waldo Emerson of his hometown, and, of course, he is right. Boston, with her streets tracing the seventeenth-century ox-and-cart paths to historic waterfronts, possesses a chaotic, old-world charm, which has proved nevertheless adaptable to the modern age. As the city has grown and evolved over 350 years, as big granite and even bigger glass and steel buildings have sprouted beside Boston's signature red brick, the infamous "crooked and narrow" streets of Boston are precisely what has kept the city human-sized, making it a rare gem among American cities: it is "America's Walking City."

Boston is also America's oldest city. With plentiful fresh water beside a deep, sheltered harbor, the spot seemed like paradise to the weary Puritans who arrived to settle in 1630 after false starts in Salem and then Charlestown. William Blackstone, whose name still marks the first row of houses (the Blackstone block), was the original European settler on the Shawmut peninsula in 1625, and he invited the struggling Puritans across the river. The settlement was originally called Trimountaine for the three hills that then marked its skyline, but the Puritans voted to rename the new city after their hometown in England: Boston. Already their aspirations were lofty; their governor preached, "we shall be as a city upon a hill. The eyes of all people are upon us…." His words would prove prophetic when it came to Boston's starring role in the American Revolution.

Bostonians heralded the beginnings of revolution when they resisted the attempts of King Charles II to force Massachusetts to become a royal colony in 1684. The king prevailed, and laws increasing taxes and restricting trade soon followed, culminating in the now-infamous series of taxes in the 1760s—the Sugar Act, the Stamp Act, the Townshend Acts. The colonists vigorously resisted and troops were called in, setting the stage for the Boston Massacre. It was in Boston where the Sons of Liberty dumped 342 chests of tea into the harbor, where lanterns were hung "one if by land and two if by sea," and Paul Revere made his famous "midnight ride" to warn of the British advance. As the revolution approached, Boston patriots such as Samuel Adams and John Hancock gave impassioned speeches in Faneuil Hall, firing up the crowd, and earning both the hall and the city the title "Cradle of Liberty."

If the end of the 1700s marked Boston as a leading political power, the 1800s ushered in an era of cultural supremacy. With business booming after the war, Boston's elite mercantile-intellectual class, the "Boston Brahmins," sparked a cultural renaissance. The "Athens of America," as they called the city, was home to the first school in the country, the first university, the first free public library, and soon became a center of education and a mecca for writers. Alcott, Emerson, Hawthorne, Thoreau, Stowe, Whitman, even Dickens and Mark Twain stopped by, and literary journals such as the *Atlantic Monthly* began publication. Bostonians also led the way in the fight to end slavery. With thousands of free African-Americans numbered among Boston's citizens, and a strong history of religious dissent, Boston became the heart of the abolitionist movement in the years leading up to the Civil War. With so much of civil and cultural importance afoot in Boston, it seems only just that some Bostonians took to exaggerating a quote by Oliver Wendell Holmes about the city, and Boston was dubbed the "Hub of the Universe."

The latter half of the nineteenth century witnessed two events that would drastically change the look of the Hub. Landlocked Boston had looked to its swamps and a plan was hatched: a massive landfill program over fifty years, trucking in rock and dirt as well as leveling off the city's hills, in order to create land out of the marshy Back Bay. By the 1880s, Boston's landmass was triple its original size. If Back Bay was a triumph of city planning, the Hub also suffered an equivalent disaster. On Saturday night, November 9th, 1872, some passers-by noticed flames in a wholesale dry-goods house. Twenty-four hours later, the heart of downtown Boston stood in ruins, sixty-five acres in all, 800 buildings. Miraculously, perhaps due to the weekend timing, only thirty-three people were killed. Nevertheless, Boston was changed forever: although much was rebuilt, the downtown was now opened to new development.

While the landscape of Boston was changing, so were the people. As railroads increasingly replaced shipping, thus diminishing the city's sway, Boston grew a reputation for provinciality and priggishness. "Banned in Boston" became a boast for avant-garde art or theater. "Beantown" was the new nickname, a reference to the local churchy righteousness (many Bostonians ate beans on Sunday, which could be cooked in advance, thus not breaking the Christian Sabbath by cooking). The end of the century saw waves of new immigrants land in Boston: Irish, Jewish, Italian, Chinese. Though initially resented by the local populace, each proved to be a breath of cosmopolitan air in the stuffy city.

Today, Boston is an amazing blend of cultures, ethnicities, and history, where red-brick colonial masterpieces nestle side-by-side with French Empire granite facades and swooping mirror-wall skyscrapers. The Hub is once again a hub. A center of education with over sixty colleges and universities, the Boston area has the highest concentration of students of any metropolitan area in the country. Proximity to universities means a supply of highly skilled labor, and high-tech firms have flocked to Boston, as have financial institutions.

Boston is a city with over 350 years of history; photography has only existed for the most recent 150 of those years. *Boston Then and Now* pairs photos from the mid-to-late 1800s with contemporary photos to tell a story of the city's architectural history. It is also a story of the city's growing historical self-awareness, a story of preservation in many instances and of demolition in others, but ultimately the story of a thriving, evolving, living "museum," America's first city, Boston.

Circa 1877. Boston on the water, as the city must have appeared to countless sailors and merchant seafarers. Taken from atop the Great Northern Grain Elevator in East Boston looking southwest, these overlapping photographs show the waterfront from Rowes to Lewis Wharf, with a backdrop of the entire city. Almost forty years before the city's first skyscraper, the Custom House Tower, was built, Boston had a skyline of low buildings punctuated by spires. The many ships and wharfside businesses reveal Boston's importance as a port city.

Today, Boston's skyline is crowded with skyscrapers. The waterfront was the city's commercial heart until this century, but it fell into decline as larger ports with milder winters grew to dominate the market. Cut off from downtown by a major highway since the 1950s, the waterfront today is undergoing revitalization. A major construction project, the "Big Dig," is underway to move the highway underground by the year 2004 and use the land above for parks and recreation. In place of the commercial warehouses of the 1800s, the wharves today hold hotels, shops, and tourist sights such as the New England Aquarium.

View from the State House cupola looking east-northeast, 1858. Most striking in this photo is Boston's identity as a bustling port, revealed in the voluminous ship traffic and monumental Federalist wharves (*far left*). The city's cultural identity is also visible. The Boston Athenæum, barely twenty years old, is the Italianate building with hipped roof at near right. The Boston Museum (*center*), actually one of the city's earliest theaters, is proudly advertised near what would become Scollay Square.

Today, in this helicopter view, downtown skyscrapers blot out the wharves. The Athenæum is barely visible, and its forty-story neighbor, the rose granite One Beacon Street, blocks the view of the Flatley Building, built on the site of the Boston Museum. Government Center replaced Scollay in the 1960s. The new City Hall sits on the red-brick plaza (center). The JFK, Saltonstall, and McCormack Buildings stand at left. The historic North End is also visible in this slightly more northern view.

Arlington Street, looking southwest from the State House cupola, circa 1869. The Common and Garden are recognizable. Back Bay is a visible marsh, but the landfill project is progressing. The broad Commonwealth Avenue, with its Parisian central mall, is underway and three famous churches are already complete: Arlington Church (1861, *left*), the Church of the Covenant (1867, *center*), and First Church (1867, *not visible*). The giant shed (*center left*), a temporary coliseum, marks the location that will become Copley Square.

Today, Back Bay is a symbol of civic pride and architectural achievement.
The landfill program lasted over fifty years and created more than 450 acres
of new land. This artificial creation allowed a carefully planned order for
streets and buildings. Back Bay today is known for its varied churches and
ornate Continental apartment blocks. At the time of Back Bay's construction, the Charles River was a polluted tidal estuary, but the Charles River
Dam of 1910 transformed it into a beautiful city lagoon and recreational area.

Looking southwest across Boston, 1890. In the right foreground stands that epitome of Boston Victorian design with its French Empire roof, Alfred Mullet's 1872 Post Office. Its fireproof exterior that helped staunch the Great Fire. Most of the surrounding buildings were built after the fire and are less than twenty years old. Exceptions include the Old City Hall and the Old South Meeting House. In the far distance, the Harvard Bridge can barely be seen crossing the Charles River.

Today, the heart of Boston's financial district fills this view. The Great Fire of 1872 wiped out the historic downtown, creating the potential for urban growth, first in granite, now in glass and steel. The Art Deco post office that replaced the Mullet building in 1933 is hidden from view by newer, taller buildings. The Boston Company Building is the dark building at far right. In distant Back Bay, the Hancock and Prudential Towers are visible.

The oldest house in Boston, built in 1680, seen here in 1895. Situated in the oldest neighborhood in Boston, on the original plot of Puritan minister Increase Mather's house (destroyed in the fire of 1676), this house was home to Paul Revere and his family during the years surrounding the Revolution. It was from this house that Revere left on his famous "midnight ride" to warn of the British advance. By the time of this photo, however, the house had become a tenement and the ground floor was a storefront for a variety of businesses, at this time, a greengrocer.

Today, the Paul Revere House actually appears older than it did one hundred years ago. In 1908, the Paul Revere Memorial Association restored it to a late seventeenth-century appearance, with overhanging jetties and leaded casements, and without the extra floor added in the early 1700s. Although the clapboard and interior are reproductions, ninety percent of the frame is original. The restored Paul Revere House is one of the most popular attractions in the city, with up to a quarter-million visitors each year. The surrounding neighborhood today is the heart of Boston's Italian community.

Adjacent to the Paul Revere House stands the Pierce/Hichborn House, the oldest surviving brick residence in Boston. Built around 1711 by glazier Moses Pierce, and later home to Paul Revere's cousin, boatbuilder Nathaniel Hichborn, by the time of this 1902 photograph, the Pierce/Hichborn House, like the Revere House beside it, had become a tenement.

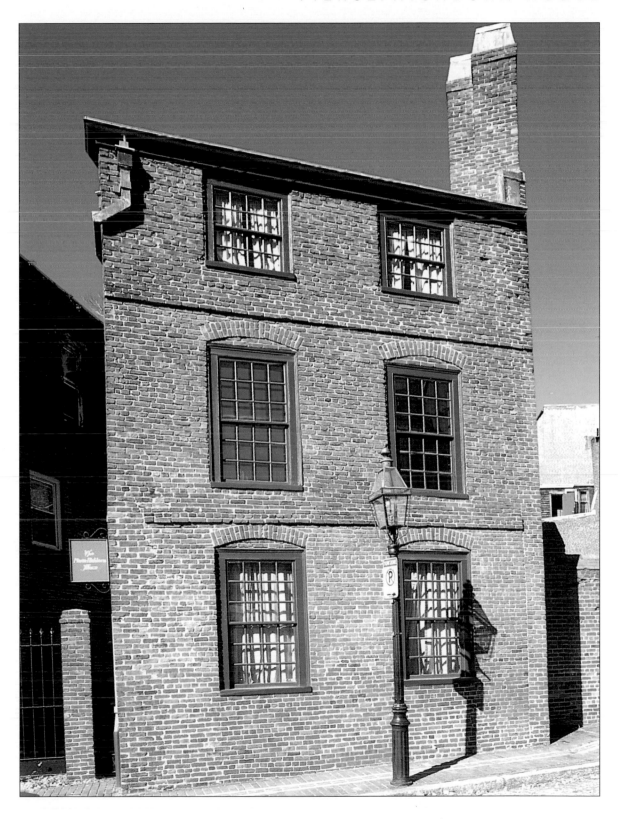

Today, after restoration in the 1950s, the property is maintained and operated by the Paul Revere Memorial Association. The house is famous as an early example of the graceful, clean-lined style, later known as Georgian, that succeeded the wood-framed Tudor stylings of Revere's house. The garden adjoining the two famous houses is also preserved as an authentic colonial herb garden.

The oldest church building in Boston, Christ Church, or Old North as it is popularly known, seen here from Hull Street, circa 1906. Designed by William Price in the style of Christopher Wren and completed in 1723, it was from Old North's nearly 200-foot steeple that church sexton Robert Newman hung the lanterns "one if by land, two if by sea" to warn colonists of British troop movements. To the left lies Copp's Hill Burying Ground, where Newman is buried along with the original Mather family, and where occupying British soldiers in 1775 used the gravestones for target practice.

Today, Old North Church remains the tallest building in the neighborhood, a rare preservation of skyline not found in contemporary downtown Boston. The steeple has been replaced twice, however, after being toppled by hurricanes in 1804 and 1954. Still inside are the church bells, cast in England in 1744, the first ever brought to America; among the first bell ringers was a fifteen-year-old Paul Revere. A peek at today's cemetery reveals a tidier Burying Ground: during the Depression, the WPA straightened and aligned the gravestones.

North Street at Lewis, circa 1868. Named for a popular London establishment, the King's Head Tavern was one of the oldest in Boston. Built most likely in the 1680s, the King's Head's proximity to the sailors on the waterfront (it was at the land end of Lewis Wharf) added to its licentious reputation, as did its carnivalesque exhibitions, including a "maiden dwarf, fifty two years old" in 1771. By the time of the Civil War, the building was in use by a boot manufacturer.

Urban renewal is not just a creation of the twentieth century: shortly after the older photo was taken, the building was torn down for civic improvement. Home in the 1600s to the original settlers and in the 1700s to the seafaring merchant class, the North End by the 1870s was in transition, as it became home to different waves of recent immigrants. Today, this area is again undergoing changes as young professionals move into this historic Italian neighborhood.

Looking west near Commercial Street at North End Beach, 1919. On an unseasonably warm January 15th, 1919, the North End witnessed a bizarre disaster: the Purity Distilling Company's fifty-foot cast-iron storage tank burst, pouring out a 2.3 million gallon tidal wave of molasses. Moving at about thirty-five miles per hour, the molasses crushed buildings (*center*) and ripped apart the elevated rail track running along Commercial Street (*twisted metal at left*). Twenty-one people and dozens of horses were drowned in the Great Molasses Flood.

Today, a plaque marks the spot where the tank once stood on the waterfront west of the North End Beach. Cleanup of the spill was a nightmare: the congealed molasses coated everything and was almost impossible to remove. Eventually, high-pressure fire hoses made some headway using saltwater from the harbor to dissolve the syrup, but a sticky residue remained for years. North-Enders still claim that the aroma lingers. The elevated rail went out of service in 1938 and was used for scrap in World War II.

Charlestown Bridge, circa 1874. First constructed in 1786 with funds raised by John Hancock and friends, the bridge was not only Boston's first, but, at forty feet, the longest in America. In 1775, the British had burned Charlestown; the bridge would help to restore the local economy. By 1874, the bridge was essential to commerce and transit, providing a quick route to Charlestown's clusters of commercial wharves (Tudor, Hittinger, etc.) and also to towns further north.

Today, Charlestown Bridge, where Washington Street crosses the mouth of the Charles River, is still a bustling connection, but, as the shipping industry has faded, so has the docks' prominence. Masted ships still dot the waterfront, but they are now mostly one-mast pleasure sailboats. The three black masts belong to the U.S.S *Constitution*, moored in Charlestown Navy Yard. The Yard was founded in 1800, but after its decommissioning in 1974, is now a National Historic Park.

U.S.S. *Constitution*, 1897. Called "Old Ironsides," not for any metal plating, but for the tough oaken hull that was seemingly impervious to bullets in the War of 1812, the U.S.S. *Constitution* is one of the six original U.S. Navy frigates. In this photograph, for the second time since commissioning in 1797, the *Constitution* was close to scuttling. Note the slapped-on extra deck and patchy paint job. The ship had been saved once before in the 1830s when Oliver Wendell Holmes' poem "Old Ironsides" spurred a preservation movement.

Today, the U.S.S. *Constitution* is the oldest commissioned ship afloat in the world. After the Navy suggested that the decrepit ship be used for target practice, public outcry led to the Constitution's restoration to its former glory. After further renovations in 1995–6, the ship celebrated its bicenten-

nial in 1997 by sailing under its own power. In a normal year, the ship makes one tour, the "turnaround" every Fourth of July, when two tugs turn the ship to ensure even wear. The U.S.S. *Constitution* is still maintained in all her three-masted glory by regular Navy personnel.

Bunker Hill Monument, circa 1870. Around midnight on June 16, 1775, colonists began building a fort on what they thought was Bunker Hill; by daylight, they realized they were atop Breed's hill. The battle was fought and the monument built there, but the misnomer remains. After eighteen years of construction, the Quincy granite obelisk was completed in 1843. The surrounding park, with its view of Boston, became the neighborhood of wealthy captains and ship owners.

Today, the Bunker Hill monument stands amid a dramatically changed Charlestown across from a dramatically changed Boston. Although the elegant 1840s row houses of Monument Square are carefully preserved, the quiet streets that surrounded the area are now overshadowed by highways and power plants. Charlestown was annexed to Boston in 1874, and the neighborhood today is working class. For those willing and able to climb the 294 steps, the monument provides sweeping views of Boston.

Boston's Long Wharf, the oldest in the city, seen here circa 1865, was also the biggest, stretching almost 2,000 feet into the harbor, from what is now State Street. Built in 1710 by Captain Oliver Noyes, Long Wharf was the cargo hub of its day, allowing safe mooring for even the deepest-drawing ships, and prompting Cunard to base the first transatlantic mail routes out of Boston in the 1840s.

Following extensive landfill and road construction in the 1950s, Long Wharf
was almost completely demolished. A few buildings were saved, including the
1763 brick warehouse where John Hancock once had an office (now a Chart
House restaurant). The granite Custom House Block was completed in 1847,
and, despite the name, has always been privately owned; it houses offices and
apartments. The boats today are mostly harbor cruisers.

India Wharf, circa 1865. Designed by Charles Bulfinch and built 1803–7, the red-brick India Wharf was one of the most ambitious undertakings in Federal Boston. Built on landfill, this row of over thirty stores, warehouses, and counting rooms, stretching almost 500 feet long and five stories high, was part of a plan to create a modern, orderly waterfront for merchants trading in the Far East, thus the name. The tip of Rowes wharf is seen at left.

Bulfinch's building was bisected by Atlantic Avenue in 1868 and completely demolished in 1962. Today, India Wharf consists of the twin forty-story Harbor Towers designed by I. M. Pei & Partners and constructed in 1971, visible at center and right. Rowes Wharf has been developed into a hotel and shopping area. Once packed with freighters and fishers, the waterfront has been transformed into a place of luxury condos, pleasure cruisers, and tourist attractions.

By 1914, the time of this photo, Long Wharf and many parts of the downtown waterfront had fallen into disrepair as traffic moved to other parts of the harbor, or to other ports altogether. Note the vacancies and lack of boat traffic. Under construction in the background stands the Custom House Tower, a federally funded project to help revitalize the area's depressed economy.

Today, most of the few remaining historic warehouses are cut off from the water by Atlantic Avenue and the Central Artery (the green elevated structure), built in the 1950s. The waterfront, however, is undergoing revitalization, and the planned rerouting of the highway underground should help. By the year 2004, the current barrier of the highway should be replaced with grassy parkland.

Above: India street, circa 1850. Designed (1847) in the style of a Greek Revival temple by architect Ammi Burnham Young, the Custom House was originally at harborside, allowing ships to tie up right outside the front door (horse at lower left was pulling away from the dock).

Right: tower construction, Peabody & Stearns, 1913–5. Funded by the federal government, the thirty-story tower atop the Custom House became Boston's first skyscraper.

Although initially considered an unattractive yoking of styles, the Custom House Tower today is a signature landmark on the Boston skyline. The tallest building in New England at the time of its construction, the 495-foot tower was permitted to surpass the city's 125-foot height limit because it was a federal building. The city bought the building in 1987, but then resold it. It is now owned by Marriott, but the viewing deck is still open to the public.

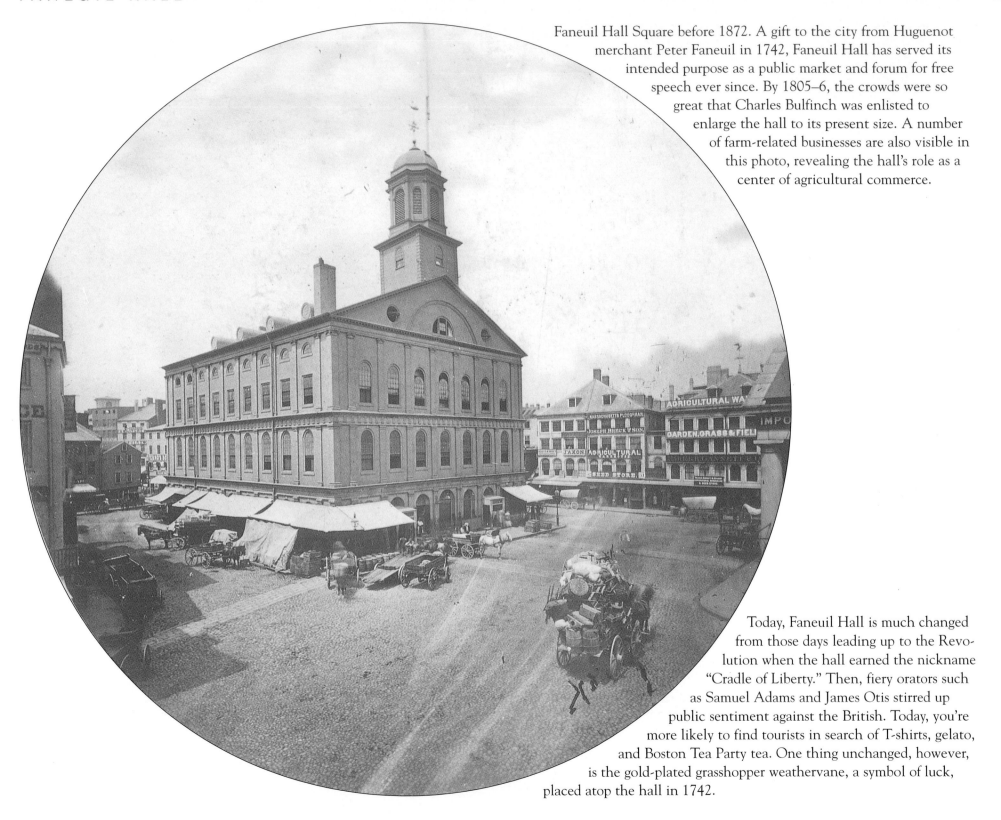

Faneuil Hall Square before 1872. A gift to the city from Huguenot merchant Peter Faneuil in 1742, Faneuil Hall has served its intended purpose as a public market and forum for free speech ever since. By 1805–6, the crowds were so great that Charles Bulfinch was enlisted to enlarge the hall to its present size. A number of farm-related businesses are also visible in this photo, revealing the hall's role as a center of agricultural commerce.

Today, Faneuil Hall is much changed from those days leading up to the Revolution when the hall earned the nickname "Cradle of Liberty." Then, fiery orators such as Samuel Adams and James Otis stirred up public sentiment against the British. Today, you're more likely to find tourists in search of T-shirts, gelato, and Boston Tea Party tea. One thing unchanged, however, is the gold-plated grasshopper weathervane, a symbol of luck, placed atop the hall in 1742.

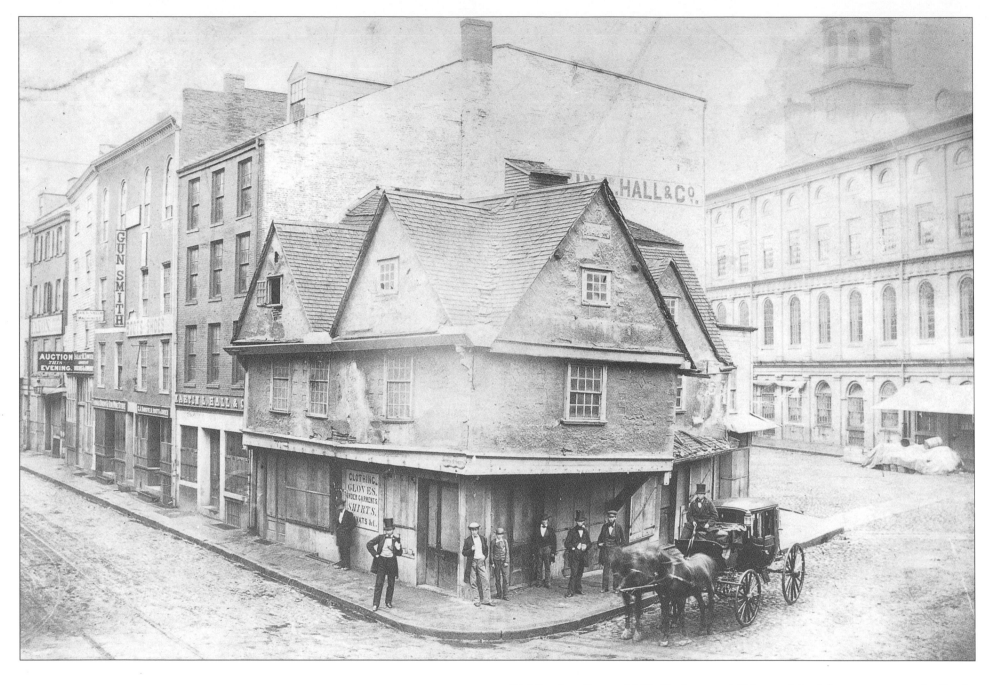

Old Feather Store, 1857. Built circa 1680, roughly the same time as the Paul Revere House and more than fifty years before Faneuil Hall (*right*), the Old Feather Store, as it came to be known late in life, served as a residence and storefront until its demolition in 1860. Its quaint Elizabethan stylings, with its overhanging jetties and multiple gables, made the store a favorite subject of painters and photographers.

Today, the Old Feather Store and her neighbors have been replaced by a glass-canopied market, designed in the late 1970s by Benjamin Thompson Associates. The multiple glass peaks of the newer structure evoke the former gabled history, but with a fresh urban twist that helped revitalize the marketplace. It's hard to believe that this was once the location of the Puritans' public dock; a sign of just how radically landfill projects have revised Boston's shoreline.

Designed by Alexander Parris in Greek Revival style, Quincy Market (1826) is not named for the Quincy granite used in its construction, but for then-mayor Josiah Quincy who proposed this extension of the Faneuil Hall Market. The project met with resistance initially, as it required the landfill of several inlets and wharves. This 1876 photo documents the market's fiftieth anniversary; a dinner in honor of the surviving original proprietors followed.

Today, consumer culture has replaced agriculture, but Quincy Market is thriving once again. As the market approached its centennial in 1976, it had fallen into decay. Architects Ben and Jane Thompson convinced the city that the market could again be vital if it were reinvented to suit contemporary urban life. Today, the interior is filled with bustling shops and cafes, and the courtyard hosts a variety of pushcart vendors and street entertainers.

On Marshall Street, 1885. Built in 1767 by John Hancock's uncle, the house was inherited by John's younger brother, Ebenezer, a paymaster in the Continental Army. From 1798 to 1963, the first floor housed the oldest continuously run shoe store in America. The round stone near street level on the building opposite the house is the Boston Stone. Once used by painter Thomas Child to grind pigments, it served as mile-marker zero for colonial Bostonians.

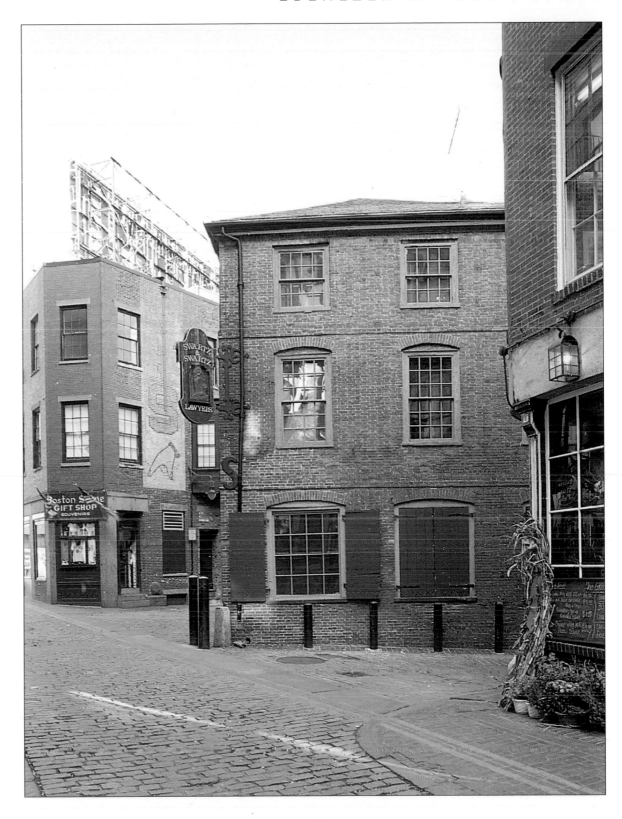

A rare surviving eighteenth-century home in downtown Boston, the Ebenezer Hancock House is restored and used today as private law offices. It is part of the Blackstone Block, one of the best preserved colonial sections of Boston, and the original area of settlement named for the Reverend William Blaxton (so he spelled it). The neighborhood was frequently under water, as is reflected in the street names: Salt Lane, Marsh Lane, Creek Square.

41–43 Union Street, circa 1880s. Built in 1714, this Georgian building was home to Hopestill Capen's dry goods store for most of the eighteenth century. Isaiah Thomas, publisher of the famous Revolutionary newspaper, *The Massachusetts Spy*, operated out of the second floor until the war began. In exile in 1797, the Duke of Chartres, future king of France, supported himself by giving French lessons from his upstairs apartment.

Still in operation today, the oldest restaurant in Boston, founded 1715, moved into the ground floor in 1826. Originally called Atwood & Bacon's (visible in the older photo), when it was located here, fishermen could sail up almost to the back door to sell their catch. Daniel Webster later became a regular customer, sometimes consuming up to three dozen oysters. In 1916, the name was changed to the Union Oyster House.

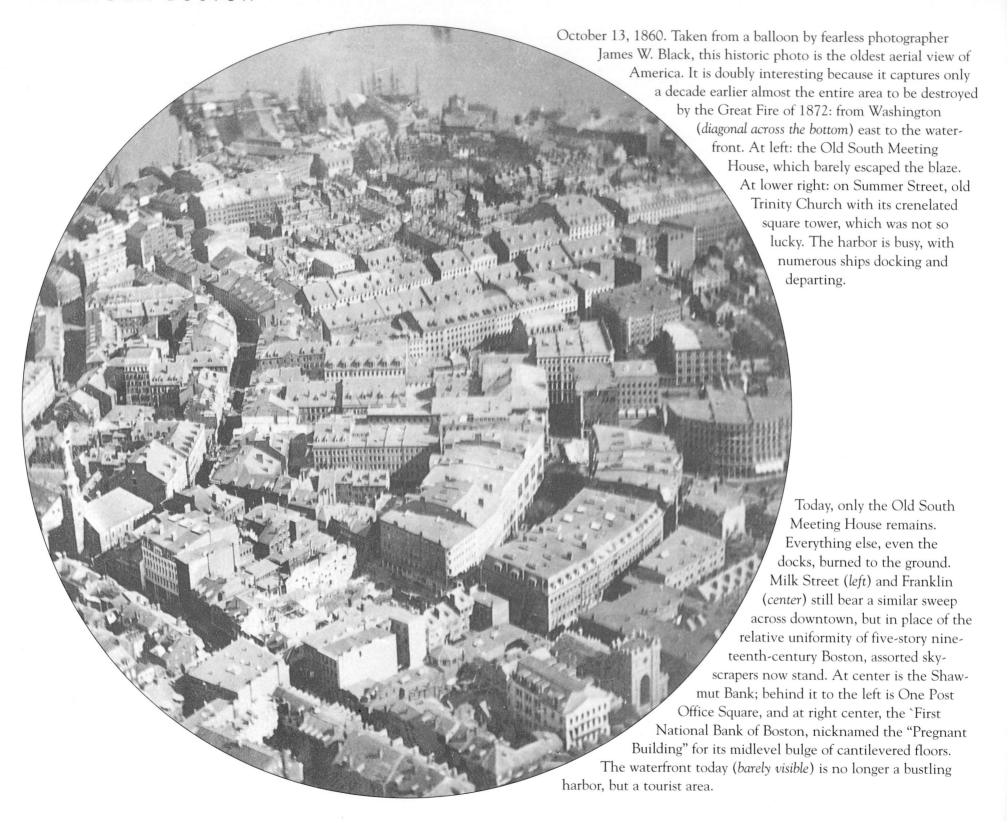

October 13, 1860. Taken from a balloon by fearless photographer James W. Black, this historic photo is the oldest aerial view of America. It is doubly interesting because it captures only a decade earlier almost the entire area to be destroyed by the Great Fire of 1872: from Washington (*diagonal across the bottom*) east to the waterfront. At left: the Old South Meeting House, which barely escaped the blaze. At lower right: on Summer Street, old Trinity Church with its crenelated square tower, which was not so lucky. The harbor is busy, with numerous ships docking and departing.

Today, only the Old South Meeting House remains. Everything else, even the docks, burned to the ground. Milk Street (*left*) and Franklin (*center*) still bear a similar sweep across downtown, but in place of the relative uniformity of five-story nineteenth-century Boston, assorted skyscrapers now stand. At center is the Shawmut Bank; behind it to the left is One Post Office Square, and at right center, the `First National Bank of Boston, nicknamed the "Pregnant Building" for its midlevel bulge of cantilevered floors. The waterfront today (*barely visible*) is no longer a bustling harbor, but a tourist area.

Between Water and Milk Streets, site of the old Post Office, 1870. This anachronistic block of houses, stables, and shops in the heart of downtown somehow managed to slip past the nineteenth-century developers for years. Soon after this photo, however, the block was chosen as the site for the new post office. During the Great Fire of 1872, the fireproof shell of the unfinished new building provided firefighters one of few safe vantage points.

After the Great Fire, the way was clear for contemporary development. Today
the area is the heart of Boston's concrete canyon. That pinnacle of Victorian
design, Alfred Mullett's Post Office from the 1870s, was replaced by the Art
Deco John W. McCormack Post Office and Court House (*left*) in 1933. In
the background, from left to right: the Fleet Bank Building, 75–100 Federal
Street, One Summer Street.

Post Office Square, 1901. The square was edged by three venerable French Second Empire buildings, constructed during the 1870s. Alfred Mullet's Victorian Post Office, giving the square its name, would have been behind the viewer. At center, stood the New York Mutual Life Insurance Building, designed by Peabody & Stearns, later architects of the Custom House Tower. The New England Mutual Life Insurance Building (1874) is at left. The buildings are draped in black to mourn the assassination of President William McKinley.

After several years inhabited by an unappealing concrete garage owned by the city, Post Office Square has been restored to the open space it was at the turn of the century. Seven levels of parking were moved underground in the 1980s. One of the rare open spaces downtown, the square offers great views of two of downtown's Art Deco buildings: the New England Telephone Building (*right*) and the McCormack Post Office (*behind the viewer*).

View down Water Street toward Washington, circa 1865. This commercial center was soon to change—the buildings at left would be torn down within five years to make way for Alfred Mullett's Post Office. Then, in the Great Fire of 1872, several of the remaining buildings burned. The street was often crowded, a situation exacerbated by the two-way buggy traffic and haphazard curbside parking.

Today, Water is a one-way street with almost no parking and little of the congestion of the previous era. The Art Deco McCormack Post Office (*left*) replaced the earlier Victorian structure in 1933. The graceful, curved edifice at center is Clarence Blackall's Winthrop Building (1893), the first steel-framed building in Boston. Across the street stand the Minot (1911) and the Fidelity Building (1906).

Summer Street and Atlantic Avenue (Dewey Square), circa 1900. When construction on this colonnaded granite building was completed around the turn of the century, the South Station was the largest train depot in the world and also the busiest, peaking in 1913 with 38 million passengers a year. South Station served trains running both west and south; prior to its construction, railroads had to build their own individual terminals.

Almost demolished entirely in the 1960s as airplanes and autos surpassed
trains in popularity, the main house of South Station today has been fully
restored on the exterior, and fully revamped on the interior. It now houses
Amtrak and commuter trains and the red line subway, in addition to shops,
coffee- and newsstands, and other services. The planning offices of the "Big
Dig," the plan to move the downtown highway underground, are located here.

Arch Street at Franklin, circa 1853. This beautiful building was the centerpiece of famed architect Charles Bulfinch's Tontine Crescent, which launched Boston's transformation from Colonial to Federal architecture. In 1794, Bulfinch built, on what used to be a quagmire, America's first block of town houses, revolutionizing how Bostonians lived and, unfortunately, bankrupting Bulfinch in the process. The Boston Library Society and the Massachusetts Historical Society occupied the rooms above the arch.

Today, the central arch of the Tontine Crescent that gave Arch Street its name is a distant memory. The entire town house row was demolished in 1858 to make way for commercial buildings. Ironically, the Great Fire of 1872 destroyed many of the new buildings soon after, but the newly commercial area was quickly rebuilt. Many of the granite buildings seen today date from the period immediately following the fire, like the five-story Renaissance building, 65 Franklin Street at right, built 1874–1875.

State Street at Devonshire, 1875. With add-on porches, mansard roof, and a slathering of signage, the Old State House is seen here at its worst, but nevertheless decked out for the American centennial. Built in 1712–1713, it served first as a meeting house for the British governor, then as a seat for the post-Revolution government until 1798 when it was replaced by Bulfinch's State House. After a period as the Boston city hall, it began a rapid decline as a common office building.

It was not until the city of Chicago tried to buy the Old State House in 1880 that Bostonians recognized the need to preserve it. The Old State House today is fully restored thanks to the Bostonian Society, organized to rescue the historic structure. It was from the balcony on the opposite end that the Declaration of Independence was first read to Bostonians on July 18th, 1776, and where six years earlier, the Boston Massacre took place in the cobblestone circle before the building.

From Scollay Square, 1856. The Old State House, decorated with multiple flags, tops the surrounding buildings. Bostonians were celebrating the 150th anniversary of native son Benjamin Franklin's birthday with a parade to City Hall, where a statue of the man was dedicated. Views of Court Street from this era are somewhat common, as many photographers had studios there. Before Court Street was widened, the face of the Old State House was hidden by adjacent buildings.

Today, the Old State House remains dignified, if, as one critic called it, a "dollhouse" in the midst of the gargantuan buildings grown up around it. The City Bank and Trust building at left takes all the curve out of the building's better back half, the Sear's Crescent. The upper left is the 35-story Bank of Boston. The building with the spiral fire escape is Boston's first granite skyscraper, the Ames building (1889). Citizens Bank at center and the dark tower of the Boston Company Building complete the picture.

State Street opposite India and the Custom House, circa 1869. Built around 1867, the building acquired its name after purchase in 1889 by Calvin Richards, a wealthy liquor merchant. The building is architecturally important because of its early foray into prefabricated construction: the facade was made in Italy, then assembled in Boston.

Today, with two additional floors and some of the original decorative iron columns removed, the Richards Building nevertheless is easily recognized. Escaping the Great Fire, which stopped at State Street, the building is the oldest surviving cast-iron building in downtown Boston and was, for a time, one of the tallest.

Washington Street, 1889. Known throughout the 1800s and into the 1900s as Newspaper Row, this stretch of Washington between State and School Streets was home not only to the illustrious *Boston Globe*, but to almost every other paper in the city. Note the bundles of newsprint on the truck in the foreground. In this scene, crowds were gathering to hear the outcome of a boxing match featuring hometown champ John L. Sullivan.

Today, the Newspaper Row of old is gone, and Washington is now home to an ordinary assortment of offices and shops. Although the scene in the historic photo is particularly congested, by the twentieth century, the traffic jams on old Boston's narrow, crooked streets were nearly constant and prevented speedy delivery of the news. The final holdout, the *Globe*, relocated in 1958.

Looking south from Milk Street, 1858. This medley of retail-row establishments in a variety of sizes and styles was typical of pre-Civil War Boston. The Great Fire of 1872 destroyed this stretch of Washington. It was from the north side of this intersection that daring citizens took to the roof of Old South with hoses in an attempt to prevent the spread of the fire.

Washington Street today is still the heart of Boston's retail row, and the buildings are still varied, only generally bigger. Straight ahead lies Downtown Crossing, a pedestrian shopping district which bills itself as New England's largest. Many of the buildings, such as Filene's, display lovely turn-of-the century civic architecture.

School Street at Washington, circa 1870s. Built in 1712 on the site of Anne Hutchinson's home (she was banished for heresy in 1637), this building was Boston's first apothecary shop until Timothy Carter, a bookseller, took over, opening the Old Corner Bookstore in 1828. The Corner became the hub of literary Boston, home to Ticknor & Fields, publisher of Emerson, Thoreau, Julia Ward Howe, Hawthorne, and the originator of the *Atlantic Monthly*.

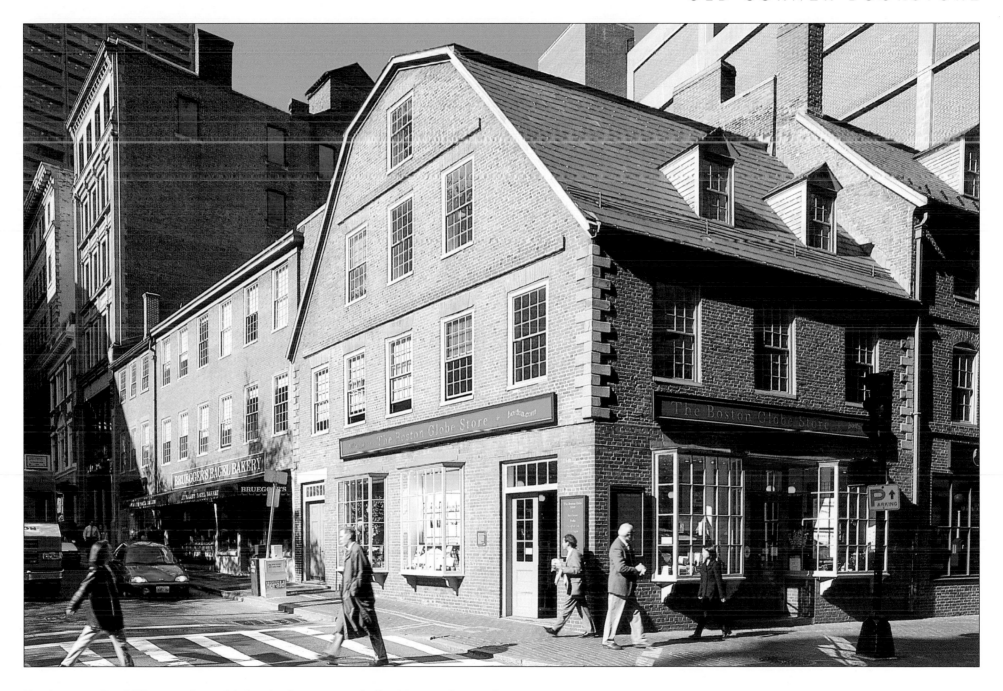

By the post-Civil War era, the publisher had outgrown the building and moved on. Targeted for demolition in the 1960s, the building survives today thanks to the efforts of a citizens' group who purchased the building and restored it to its 1828 appearance. Home for a time to the offices of the *Boston Globe*, the building was reopened as the Globe Corner Bookstore in 1982, but now stands as the Boston Globe Store. Newer buildings now block the view of the Old City Hall.

School Street near Tremont, circa 1895. Built during the Civil War and designed by Back Bay planner Arthur Gilman, the Old City Hall is a fine example of French Second Empire architecture, with its copper-plated mansard in the style of the Louvre. The building was city hall in the heyday of the Boston political machine, when oft-elected Mayor James Michael Curley referred to his office on the second floor as "Agony Corner." Statues of Josiah Quincy and Ben Franklin grace the entrance.

Today, Old City Hall is hailed as an early example of "adaptive re-use," the recycling of outdated public buildings championed in the 1960s. After the new Government Center City Hall took over its function, Old City Hall was redesigned to hold offices, restaurants, and, appropriately, the Boston Preservation Alliance. The statues still mark the entrance, although hidden by the fencing and landscaping added earlier this century. The Boston Company Building now stands in the background.

Tremont Street at School, circa 1870s. King's Chapel stands on the site of the first Anglican church in the colonies, that is, on a corner of Boston's oldest cemetery. In 1688, Puritans so opposed the construction of this church of their oppressors that they would not sell their land to the colony's governor, so he seized this corner of public land to build a wooden church. The granite replacement was assembled around the original structure to avoid interruption of services, and the old church was then dismantled from within and removed through the windows.

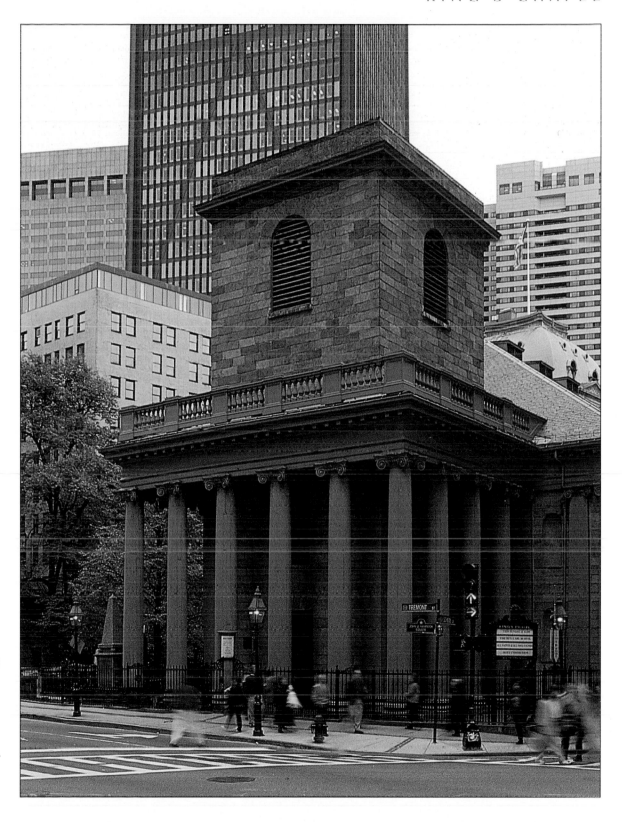

Funds ran out before architect Peter Harrison's spire could be built, so this squat Georgian chapel in Quincy granite was as complete as it would ever be by 1754. Today, thanks to the boxy buildings in the background, King's Chapel seems less truncated, more complete. The only substantial change in the Chapel itself has been a philosophical one: after the Revolutionary War, in a rejection of all things British, the congregation elected to become the first American Unitarian church in 1789. The Old City Hall peaks over the Chapel in both eras.

Washington Street at Milk Street, 1876. The second oldest church in Boston (after Old North), Old South was built in 1729 as both a house of worship and a town hall, and later became famous as a hotbed of Revolutionary oratory and the launch point for the Boston Tea Party. It was in retaliation for the latter, that the British commandeered the meeting house during their occupation of the city, stripping the interior, and housing their cavalry within. The congregation returned after the war, but relocated to New Old South in Back Bay in the 1870s.

By the time of the old photo, Old South was a decrepit post office in danger of demolition. Having escaped the Fire of 1872, the building might not have escaped the developers had it not been for the Old South Preservation Committee. Their banners are seen in the photo: "Never before in history has there been a nation base enough to destroy its own monuments...." Today, the Old South Meeting House contains a permanent history exhibit. Cars replace streetcars, and the Devonshire Towers and the Exchange Place loom overhead.

Winter Street looking toward Summer, circa 1860. Mid-nineteeth-century Summer Street, with its convenient proximity to the Common and the shops on Washington Street, was a desirable mixed commercial-residential neighborhood. The original Trinity Church is glimpsed in the distance. All was destroyed in the fire of 1872, and the commercial district took over.

Taken from Tremont Street just a half-century later in 1913, this view shows the huge commercial changes in post-fire Boston. In the distance is the newly constructed Filene's, an eight-story Beaux-Arts style department store. Men and women crowd the sidewalks and spill out into the street, but the policeman at center is unperturbed by the jaywalking.

By the 1970s, this shopping district was renamed Downtown Crossing and made an official pedestrian mall. The area is still bustling with storefronts and restaurants and now even larger department stores. The beautiful terracotta facade of Filene's still glows in the distance at right, but competitor department store Jordan Marsh, another old Boston fixture holding down the opposite corner for well over one hundred years, is now a Macy's.

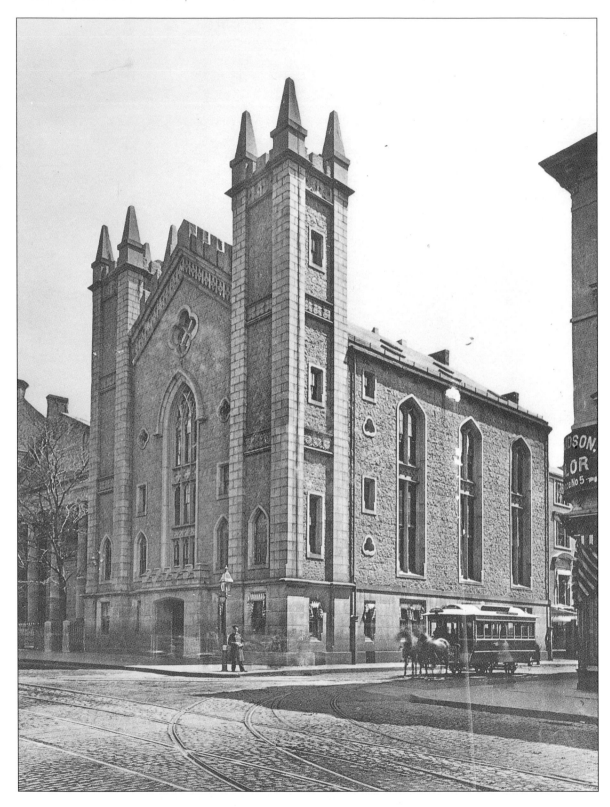

Masonic Temple at Tremont Street, circa 1860. Built in 1830–1832, this great Gothic structure that gave the side street its name is where Emerson began his career as a lecturer. A Temple School for children was established in 1834, taught by Bronson Alcott, father of Louisa, and Elizabeth Peabody, one of the city's prominent nineteenth-century intellectuals.

After the Masons built a new temple on Tremont at Boylston in the 1850s, the Gothic building became a federal courthouse, but was eventually torn down. Today, a towering commercial building marks the spot, dwarfing St. Paul's Episcopal next-door (*left*), Boston's first true example of the Greek Revival style, built in 1819–20. The architect, Alexander Parris, later designed Quincy Market.

Circa 1865. Named for the original landmark Masonic temple on the corner at Tremont (*previous page*), Temple Place became one of the most desirable residential streets in downtown in the later 1800. A so-called "ladder" street between Washington and Tremont, Temple Place offered the quiet beauty of the Common, yet convenient proximity to the increasing bustle of the Washington Street shops.

Today, the commercial district has replaced most of the residential areas. Although the Great Fire of 1872 stopped at Washington, Temple Street nevertheless was completely rebuilt in the post-fire boom. A few venerable old Boston businesses are now located here (Stoddard's cutlery, Simpson's jewelers, Santacross Shoes), but little of the mid-nineteenth century neighborhood remains.

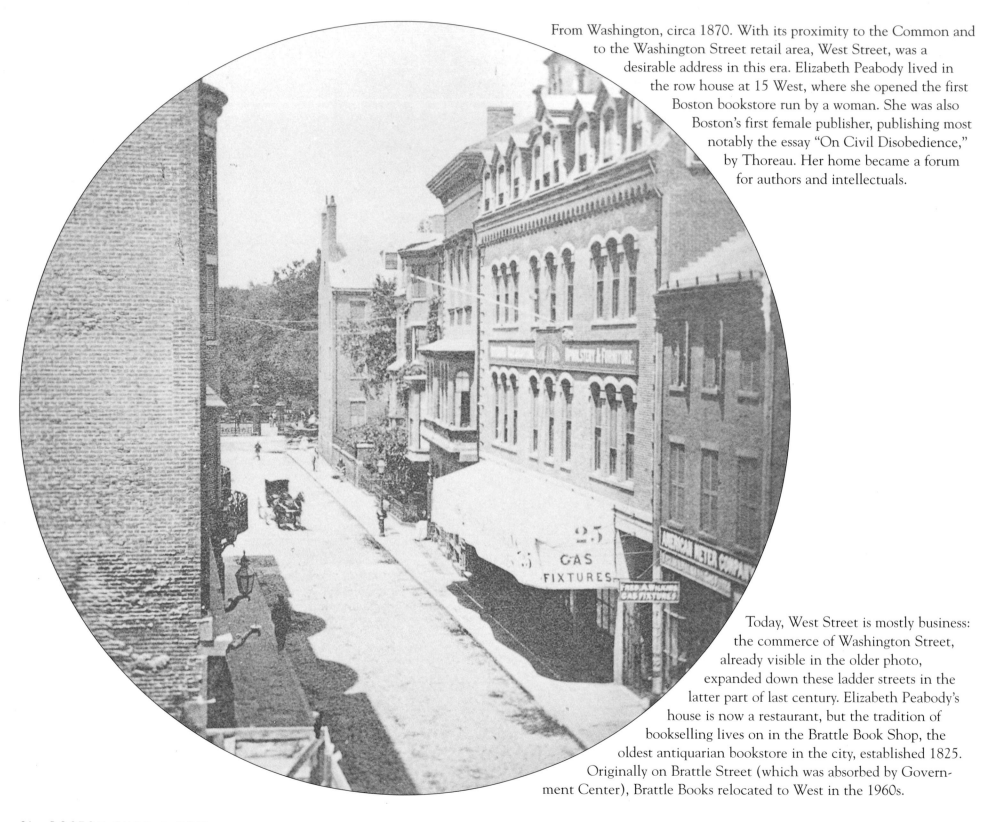

From Washington, circa 1870. With its proximity to the Common and to the Washington Street retail area, West Street, was a desirable address in this era. Elizabeth Peabody lived in the row house at 15 West, where she opened the first Boston bookstore run by a woman. She was also Boston's first female publisher, publishing most notably the essay "On Civil Disobedience," by Thoreau. Her home became a forum for authors and intellectuals.

Today, West Street is mostly business: the commerce of Washington Street, already visible in the older photo, expanded down these ladder streets in the latter part of last century. Elizabeth Peabody's house is now a restaurant, but the tradition of bookselling lives on in the Brattle Book Shop, the oldest antiquarian bookstore in the city, established 1825. Originally on Brattle Street (which was absorbed by Government Center), Brattle Books relocated to West in the 1960s.

At West, circa 1850. Another great urban design by Charles Bulfinch, Colonnade Row numbered nineteen four-story houses overlooking the Common, stretching from West Street south to Avery. Completed in 1811, and deemed by contemporaries Bulfinch's best work, the houses soon filled with "Boston's best." By the era of this photo, the uniform roofline and facades had been altered, and the Row was in decline.

The 1850s were unkind to the legacy of Charles Bulfinch; two of his greatest residential designs were then destroyed in the name of commerce and progress—the Tontine Crescent in 1858 (page 58) and Colonnade Row in 1855. Today, this block contains high-rise apartments with street-level stores, most built in the 1960s and 70s. Tremont-on-the-Common is the building with the balconies; beyond it stands the Parkside.

Washington Street in its heyday, circa 1930s. During the pre-Depression golden age of theater and throughout the 1930s and 40s, this stretch of Washington between West and Boylston displayed a row of handsome theaters and theater hotels. RKO Keith's movie palace (*right*) was originally the B. F. Keith Memorial Theater, built in 1927–1928 to honor the show-biz innovator who literally invented vaudeville.

Today, these registered historic places are in sad shape. After a brief stint as
The Savoy, Keith's finally became known as the Opera House while hosting
Sarah Caldwell's Boston Opera Company. Unfortunately, the building has
been dark since 1991. Both the Opera House, with its Baroque terra-cotta
facade, and its stunning Art Deco neighbor, the Paramount (built 1932, *left*)
are still awaiting restoration.

Southwest corner, circa 1860. The Pelham Hotel was built in 1857, as the so-called "first apartment house in America." Its Parisian-inspired design by Alfred Stone, with each flat consisting of a horizontal suite of rooms (called a "French flat"), was seen as a tremendous innovation to Bostonians accustomed their vertical, multistory town houses. The mansard roof and street-level cafe were additional French touches.

Today, the Gothic-inspired Little Building at 80 Boylston occupies this corner. Designed in 1916 by Clarence Blackall, it was one of the most prestigious buildings of the early 1900s, with its own subway access and an indoor arcade of shops. In the foreground, the Boylston Street Station is now visible due to the 1869 widening of Tremont Street. The Hotel Pelham was slid off its foundation and moved back thirty feet.

Looking east, 1870. With its graceful arched windows facing the Boston Common is the first Boston Public Library, completed in 1858 to Charles Kirby's Italianate design. Founded in 1852, the library was the first major American collection free to the public. This section of Boylston between Tremont and Charles was then known as Piano Row for its concentration of piano-making and music-publishing businesses.

Today, this stretch of Boylston is home to luxury hotels and theaters. The BPL relocated to Back Bay in 1895, and the Colonial Building now marks its former location. Built in 1900 by Clarence Blackhall, who also designed some dozen other Boston theaters, this ten-story office building holds the immaculately preserved Colonial Theater, still showing major productions today.

Hamilton Place off Tremont, 1896. Built in 1852, the Music Hall was state of the art, with seats for 2,000 and a new system of gas lighting. The Boston Symphony Orchestra debuted here in 1881. A variety of famous lecturers also spoke, from Emerson to Booker T. Washington and Oscar Wilde. Cultural businesses surrounded the Hall: book and print shops and an office for the now-forgotten art of oratory.

By the 1930s, the Music Hall had been transformed into Loew's Orpheum Theater, a vaudeville and later movie theater. The surrounding businesses lost the aura of culture; the old bookstore in the Phillips Building (built 1883, *left*) turned into a Woolworth's. Today, the hall is known simply as the Orpheum Theater, and it is once again a live music venue, showing the occasional pop or rock music concert.

Near Scollay Square on Tremont Street, circa 1890s. Designed by Hammatt Billings and built in 1846, the so-called Boston Museum was actually one of Boston's earliest theaters, its name a nod to Puritan distaste for the depravity, and later Brahmin distaste for the vulgarity, of such pursuits. The main stage was euphemistically called the Lecture Hall.

Today, the Flatley Building stands at 18 Tremont Street, housing offices and cafes catering to the nearby governmental clientele. The impressive four-story granite Boston Museum was torn down in 1903, just a few years after the historic photo. At its height of popularity in the 1880s, it held 1,200 seats, and ticket prices ranged from thirty-five cents to a dollar.

Toward Tremont, circa 1869. At center stands the original Scollay Building, named for early Boston booster, apothecary William Scollay. It was demolished in 1871 for street widening, officially creating Scollay Square. This intersection, with streets leading to the waterfront, Beacon Hill, and the South End, was always busy.

From Court Street, 1884. After the street widening, Scollay Square became a major transportation hub. The horsecars of the Union Railway operated between Cambridge and Boston; electric trolley cars were not introduced until 1889. The subway was built in the late 1890s, and by 1905, two of the city's four subway lines crossed here. The statue is Boston's founder John Winthrop, later moved to a more restful location in First and Second Church, Back Bay.

Today, Scollay Square is the heart of Government Center. By the twentieth century, the Square had become infamous for its seedy nightlife, tattoo parlors, cheap hotels, and all-night theaters. In the 1960s, the city completely demolished the area to create an open plaza hemmed by formal concrete buildings. The cobblestone island marks roughly where the original Scollay Building stood. The Center Plaza Crescent is on the left, and other government buildings, including the new City Hall (*just out of view*) at right. The twin towers of the JFK Federal Building loom overhead.

Howard Street, circa 1910s. Just around the block from Scollay Square proper, stood the Old Howard. A Millerite temple once held this spot, but in 1846, this Gothic stone structure replaced it. The new theater, called the Howard Athenæum, featured the first Italian opera ever performed in Boston. By the early 1900s, the Old Howard, as it came to be known, had descended to the ranks of novelty theater, featuring vaudeville, burlesque, and eventually striptease. "Something was always doing" at the Howard, went the slogan.

Today, the location of the former Old Howard is approximately in the midst of the open space behind Center Plaza Crescent. The Old Howard burned down in 1961, but the area had already been targeted for redevelopment. Famed architect I. M. Pei was hired to design the master plan. In the end, twenty-two streets were removed, along with their buildings, including Brattle, Cornhill, and Howard Streets. The result is the formal, concrete-lined plaza of Government Center.

Looking south, circa 1875. Once a high hill (significantly reduced by an 1835 landfill project), Pemberton Square was designed, and auctioned to Boston's finest citizens soon thereafter, by Patrick Tracy Jackson. Pemberton Square had an even older history: it was the seventeenth-century homestead of Reverend John Cotton, original Puritan rector of St. Botolph's church in Lincolnshire.

One of only two parks on Beacon Hill, Pemberton Square is long gone, fallen to the spread of downtown. Today, in its place, there is only an open plaza in the midst of big buildings adjacent to Government Center: the old Suffolk County Courthouse (1893; *right*), One Beacon (*center*), and the Center Plaza Crescent (1968; *left*). Plaques around the square are the only hints of its 350-year history.

Looking toward Somerset Street, 1889. A century before this photo was taken, the "Brahmin Land" of upper Beacon was already home to some of Boston's most esteemed, including John Hancock, Governor Bowdoin, and Reverend William Emerson (father of Ralph). In 1839, the Boston Athenæum (founded 1807) moved into the Renaissance Venetian-style palazzo designed by Edward Clark Cabot (*right center*). The block was also home to the newlywed Isabella Stewart Gardner and the exclusive Somerset Club.

Today, the still-resident Boston Athenæum now nestles between taller structures. The 1898 Congregational House (*near right*) features four facade carvings of scenes from New England history such as the Mayflower Compact and John Eliot preaching to the Indians. However, it is the polished pink granite tower of One Beacon, built in 1972, that now dominates upper Beacon, reminding us of the financial and government districts just around the corner from what was once a very exclusive residential address.

A view of the State House, 1860s. Built 1795–7, this graceful State House in the Federalist style is perhaps the finest surviving contribution to Boston by celebrated architect Charles Bulfinch. The area was still considered "country," but this stylish new capitol helped lure wealthy Bostonians to Beacon Hill. The dome was covered in gray-painted copper sheeting installed by Paul Revere & Sons in 1802; it was not gilded until 1874.

The 23-karat gilded dome of the State House today still glitters atop Beacon Hill. It has only once been dimmed, to thwart the threat of air raids in World War II. The building has expanded dramatically: a disproportionately long rear section was added in the 1890s. To reestablish the harmony of the original, the wings were added in 1914–7. The essential structure of the building has remained unchanged since that final addition.

View from the State House grounds, circa 1858. Originally the city outskirts, Park Street was once home to a poorhouse, a jail, and an insane asylum. By the early 1800s, however, Charles Bulfinch had completed the State House at the top of the street and a series of prestigious residences facing the Common that became known as Bulfinch Row. Park Street Church followed in 1809, as the neighborhood filled with well-to-do Bostonians.

Of Bulfinch's creations, only the Amory-Ticknor house survives. It is still rec-ognizable on the corner, although its former Federal beauty has been dimin-ished by later modifications. Next-door, two nineteenth-century buildings joined together house the Union Club, founded 1863, one of Boston's most prestigious private clubs. So lofty in the older photo, the Park Street Church spire is now backed by New Boston skyscrapers.

Early twentieth-century view of Park Street. "Perfectly felicitous" was Henry James's depiction of the 217-foot steeple atop the Christopher Wren-inspired Park Street Church. It was designed by English architect Peter Banner and built in 1810 on the grounds of an old granary. Recognizable at center is the Park Street Station, where the first American subway opened in 1897.

Restored to its original red brick, the Park Street Church holds the title of "most interesting mass of brick and mortar in America," again compliments of Henry James. However, the church no longer dominates the skyline: One Beacon towers in the background. Just beyond the church at street level, trees grace the Old Granary Burying Ground.

Construction of Park Street Station, circa 1896. Despite its illustrious history (in 1829, Garrison made his first antislavery speech here), the Park Street Church in this era had such financial difficulties that the basement had to be rented out as a tearoom. This section of the Common quickly became a favorite promenade. America's first subway was launched from the Park Street Station on September 1st, 1897, exchanging promenade for progress.

Tremont Street Mall is again a bustling center of activity, both for business and recreation. One Beacon (*left*) and the Boston Company Building (*right*) have sprouted beyond the Park Street Church. The entrance to Park Street Station today is the original kiosk; however, the "T" below has expanded drastically beyond its first two stops on either side of the Common to include service to Cambridge, Charlestown, Brookline, and the airport.

Looking east, 1870. Once pastureland belonging to artist John Singleton Copley, the west slope of Beacon Hill was quickly transformed into a locus of Boston Brahmin power and prestige after falling into speculators' hands in 1774. "The sunny street that holds the sifted few," as denizen Oliver Wendell Holmes characterized it, Beacon Street owes much of its elite status to the unhindered view across the Common. The fifty-acre Common (*right*) was already a venerable institution by the date of this photo, cattle grazing having been outlawed forty years earlier.

Beacon Street today retains much of the flavor of Old Boston: the Federalist brick row houses, often with classic Boston bow-fronts, remain unchanged. The Beacon Hill Architectural Commission helps preserve the historic appearance, down to the gaslamps and brick sidewalks. The Boston Com-

mon, recognized today as the oldest public park in America, is still the heart of Boston, just as one hundred years ago. Contemporary Boston creeps in, however, toward the end of Beacon Street, where downtown skyscrapers, One Beacon and the Boston Company Building, crowd the view.

From Pinckney Street, around 1895. The patrician bow-front houses of Louisburg Square (built in the 1830s) follow the original Charles Bulfinch plan of 1826, although at two-thirds the original size. "We are quite a literary precinct," wrote noted editor/author William Dean Howells about this elite slice of Beacon Hill. Other literary notables who lived nearby: Louisa May Alcott, Henry James, and later, for a time, Robert Frost.

Today, Louisburg Square remains virtually unchanged. The central parkland is still commonly owned by the Louisburg Square Proprietors, America's first homeowners' association. The only park remaining on Beacon Hill (there was one other, page 102), Louisburg Square remains a posh address, although somewhat without the glamor of the late 1800s when famous authors, artists, and singers made their homes here.

Smith Court, circa 1860. Probably designed by noted architect Asher Benjamin and certainly built in his town-house style in 1806 by free African-American artisans, the African Meeting House is the oldest standing black church in the United States. In 1832, famed abolitionist William Lloyd Garrison founded here the New England Anti-Slavery Society with its demand for immediate emancipation, thus earning the structure its nickname, "the Black Faneuil Hall."

The African Meeting House was opened to the public in 1987 as part of the Museum of Afro-American History. For most of the 1800s, it served as church, school, and community center for Boston's African-Americans, most of whom lived on the north slope of Beacon Hill. Toward the end of the nineteenth century, the neighborhood changed to predominantly Irish, then Jewish, and the Meeting House was used as a synagogue until its restoration began in 1972.

Cambridge Street, 1916. The first of three houses built by Charles Bulfinch for lawyer Harry Otis, who would later become mayor. Built in 1796, Otis only lived here at the foot of Beacon Hill for four years. By the time of this photo, the formerly elegant Federalist mansion had been converted to storefronts. The Old West Church next-door, designed by Asher Benjamin (1806), was in use as a public library branch.

Today, the Otis House is restored to its late eighteenth-century splendor, thanks to the Society for the Preservation of New England Antiquities now headquartered there. The Old West Church, also restored, is now a Methodist church. The rest of the nearby area did not fare so well when it fell into disrepair; the city demolished the entire Old West End in the 1960s to make way for Government Center.

From Cambridge, 1864. The West Boston Bridge (1794) provided the quickest means to Cambridge from Boston. The Charles River itself provided another route when frozen over. The domed State House crowns Beacon Hill, to its right is the faint Park Street Church spire. On the waterfront from left to right, the Massachusetts Eye and Ear Infirmary stands beside the octagonal gasworks of the Boston Gaslight Company. To the left of the bridge is the Massachusetts General Hospital (*far left*) and the hulking Charles Street Jail.

Today, the big buildings of new Boston overshadow Beacon Hill. The Massachusetts General Hospital and the Eye and Ear Infirmary are still there, although in new buildings. The waterfront has become a center of recreation, rather than commerce, with the boathouse for scullers and sailors, and the

Hatch Memorial Shell for outdoor concerts. Today, the Longfellow Bridge (1907) occupies roughly the same location as the old West Boston. It is also called the salt-and-pepper bridge for its mini-tower finials resembling salt shakers.

Looking west, 1870. In 1870, the "flat" of Beacon Hill, so-called for the level ground leading east to the hill, was also leading the way west to the newly filled land in Back Bay. The Public Garden by this date was already a favorite promenade for Victorian Bostonians. It is hard to believe it was once on the edge of the dry Common, a marshy patch, flooded by the Charles River, and hemmed by rope footbridges.

Today, the vast horizon stretching to Back Bay has filled in with cars, trees, people. The brick sidewalks and row houses now mingle with newer (and bigger) buildings. Over one hundred years later, the Public Garden remains an enduring green space in the heart of the city. Site of the first tulips ever planted in the United States, the Garden contains a meandering four-acre lake, home to the famous swan boats.

Boylston Street at Arlington, on the edge of civilization, 1862. Completed in 1861 in the graceful style of Christopher Wren, the Arlington Street Church was the first building to be erected in Back Bay. Until the launch of an ambitious landfill project in 1857, Back Bay was a marshy wasteland. By the end of the century, it would be the darling of Boston's elite, a showcase for the best of Victorian architecture, and an extra 450 acres of land for the crowded city.

Today, Arlington Street marks the transition from the crooked cowpaths of eighteenth-century Boston to the broad, Parisian-inspired boulevards of nineteenth-century Back Bay. Architect Arthur Gilman designed the orderly layout for the streets and the Arlington Street Church too. This Unitarian church has a history of political engagement from abolition to the peace movement. The neighborhood today is packed with shops, offices, and apartments.

Dartmouth Street, 1869. It is almost impossible to imagine that this quickly thrown together, warehouse-like structure, Boston's largest indoor auditorium at the time, stood on what was rapidly becoming Copley Square. Standing in the midst of the enormous Back Bay landfill project, the Peace Jubilee Coliseum hosted a national peace celebration at the end of the Civil War.

On the exact location at Dartmouth and St. James now stands the luxury
Copley Plaza Hotel, host to gala social events, presidents, and royalty since
its opening in 1912. The hotel actually took over the spot vacated previously
by the original Museum of Fine Arts, which moved from its cramped Back
Bay location there to the Fenway in 1909. At left, the Hancock Tower.

Circa 1885. Over a sparse Copley Square, Trinity church rises on 4,500 pilings to support it in the gravel landfill. Designed by Henry Hobson Richardson, this masterpiece of French-Romanesque style (now known as Richardson Romanesque), completed in 1877, was the second major con-struction project on the square. At right is the old Museum of Fine Arts, built in Ruskinian Gothic style in 1876. At center, it appears that ground is already being prepared for the Public Library.

Today, Trinity Church is a National Historic Landmark overlooking a bustling Copley Square. On the right stands the Copley Plaza Hotel; beyond it, the mirrored, sixty-two story John Hancock Tower, an acclaimed design by I. M. Pei & Partners in 1976. Behind the Hancock Tower is the Art Deco

Hancock Building, Boston's tallest when it was completed in 1949. Directly behind Trinity, the 500 Boylston Building was erected in 1988, despite a citizens' attempt to block its construction.

Henry N. Cobb, Architect

Copley Square, 1880. Completed in 1875, this Northern Italian Gothic church became the new home of the Old South Meeting House congregation. Beyond it, houses were slowly filling in Dartmouth Street out toward Newbury. In a little over ten years, the grassy plaza before the church would be taken up by the new library.

Today, the great tower of the church is still a Copley Square landmark; however, it is shorter than the original. In the 1930s, the tower was found to be leaning, due to a combination of the soft fill of Back Bay and the construction of the Boylston Street subway station. The tower was replaced with a smaller one, a subtle change thanks to reuse of the original stone.

Library construction, 1889. Despite the diagonal road before Trinity Church creating two triangles of lawn, this area was already known as Copley Square and the new library helped finalize its shape. Completed in 1895, this new library, designed by Charles McKim in the Italian Renaissance Revival style, marked the shift of Boston's cultural center from the historic old city to the broad vistas and tall spires of Back Bay.

Today, the Boston Public Library is the second largest in the country, serving over two million people yearly. With the completion of the Library, Copley Square was essentially complete. The bisecting road was finally removed in 1969, creating an actual square of the Square. Trinity Church is barely seen behind the Library. Above it, the Art Deco Hancock Building and the sleek Hancock Tower. At left, the tower of Old New South.

Marlborough Street at Berkeley Street, 1880. Built in 1867, the First Church of Boston was the fifth successive meeting house of Boston's first Puritan congregation; this photo commemorates their 250th anniversary. The church was designed by William Ware and Henry Van Brunt and built of puddingstone with brown stone trim in an English Gothic style. The statue of city founder John Winthrop stands on the Marlborough side.

Today, the First and Second Church of Boston (the congregations joined in 1970) is an architectural hybrid. The First Church was almost completely destroyed by fire in 1968. The arcade entrance and the badly damaged steeple were all that remained, and they were incoporated into the new design. The building at left is the ten-story Haddon Hall apartment house (1894), the first tall building in Back Bay.

CHRISTIAN SCIENCE MOTHER CHURCH

Mary Baker Eddy's "prayer in stone," the original First Church of Christ, Scientist (*left*) was built in 1894 of rough granite in a Romanesque style, but it would not stay modest for long. By 1906 (*below*), a massive expansion was underway: the addition, a composite of Byzantine and Romanesque styles by architect Charles Brigham with a towering dome, would seat 3,000.

Today, both modest Romanesque church and Byzantine expansion are part of the Christian Science International Headquarters complex. In 1973, I. M. Pei designed a twenty-two-acre campus of buildings (*left*) to house the church's publishing society (originator of the *Christian Science Monitor*) and administration. Formerly located on the outer limits of Boston respectability, the church has witnessed the slow growth of the city to meet Eddy's vision.

Circa 1905. The newly completed Symphony Hall (1900; *left*) in this photo was the dream of Brahmin philanthropist Henry Lee Higginson, who founded the Boston Symphony Orchestra in 1881. He commissioned McKim, Mead, & White (architects also of the BPL) to design this Italianate hall for the orchestra, when the downtown Music Hall seemed unviable. The Horticultural Hall (1901) sits in the center, considered the best example of English Baroque in Boston.

Today, Symphony Hall is still internationally famous for its acoustics, which have led listeners to call it the "Stradivarius" of concert halls. It was the first hall to be built according to principles of acoustical engineering newly developed by a professor at the Massachusetts Institute of Technology. The Horticultural Hall also stands today, housing the Horticulture Society's library. The cable cars along Huntington were replaced by the green subway line.

Governor's Square, 1914. Much earlier it was known as Sewall's Point, the only dry land in the tidal salt marsh that, when landfilled, became Back Bay. From it's inception in the late nineteeth century, this intersection where three major arteries meet, Beacon (*right*), Commonwealth (*left*), and Brookline (*far right*), was always busy. The building at center is the 1911 Peerless Motor Car Building, an early automotive showroom.

Known since 1932 as Kenmore Square, this intersection is still a critical junction, now for subways rather than streetcars. The sixty-foot square neon Citgo sign, perched atop the old Peerless Building, dates from 1965. When threatened with demolition in 1982, locals successfully fought to preserve the Pop Art hit. The area is now home to Boston University and thousands of students. The Peerless houses the university bookstore.

INDEX